D0498048

A WHO HQ GRAPHIC NOVEL

Who Is Tibet's Exiled Leader?

THE 14TH DALAI LAMA

To Natascha Morris who turned me from reader to writer
in the GN realm, and to Rachel Sonis for her incredible
patience and kindness in guiding me through that realm—TR

To EC, FG, WS, and my mom—AP

PENGUIN WORKSHOP
An imprint of Penguin Random House LLC, New York

First published in the United States of America by Penguin Workshop,
an imprint of Penguin Random House LLC, New York, 2023

Visit us online at penguinrandomhouse.com.

Library of Congress Cataloging-in-Publication Data is available.

Manufactured in Italy

ISBN 9780593384589 (pbk)   10 9 8 7 6 5 4 3 2 1 LEG
ISBN 9780593384602 (hc)   10 9 8 7 6 5 4 3 2 1 LEG

Lettering by Comicraft
Design by Jay Emmanuel

This is a work of nonfiction. All of the events that unfold in the narrative
are rooted in historical fact. Some dialogue and characters have been fictionalized
in order to illustrate or teach a historical point.

The publisher does not have any control over and does not assume
any responsibility for author or third-party websites or their content.

For more information about your favorite historical figures, places, and events,
please visit whohq.com.

A WHO HQ GRAPHIC NOVEL

Who Is Tibet's Exiled Leader?
THE 14TH DALAI LAMA

by Teresa Robeson
illustrated by Angela Poon

Penguin Workshop

Introduction

In the spring of 1959, thousands of Tibetans flocked to Lhasa, the capital city of Tibet, for Monlam Chenmo, the Great Prayer Festival, and to catch a glimpse of their beloved leader, the Dalai Lama. The Precious Protector, as he was often called, was set to make his usual public appearance during the celebration.

At just twenty-three years old, the Dalai Lama might seem a bit young to be the leader of six million Tibetan people. But it's a role he was born into: The Dalai Lama (born Lhamo Thondup) had held the "job" of spiritual leader since he was four, and was officially crowned political leader at fifteen. In fact, at the time of the festival, he was in the middle of finishing up his final exams for his doctorate degree in Buddhist Studies at Lhasa's Jokhang Temple—a joyous conclusion of his studies for the highest monastic degree.

The problem was that this year's Monlam wasn't quite as joyous. Tibetans had been upset ever since 1950 when Communist leader Chairman Mao Zedong in neighboring China sent the People's Liberation Army (PLA) across the border to occupy Tibetan towns. China claimed that Tibet used to be a part of China and should be again. They forced Tibetan officials to sign a document called the "Seventeen-Point Agreement," which granted China the right to rule Tibet. Tibetans, however, didn't want to be ruled by a foreign government, and protesters fought back in towns near the Eastern border. In fact, many Tibetans from that region also fled the fighting and came to Lhasa in fear and outrage.

Tensions were running high. The PLA had headquarters right outside of the capital city, and the thousands of citizens gathering within Lhasa for the festival felt angry and nervous about what would happen next to their country. Because of this, the Dalai Lama's chief of security, Phuntsog Tashi Taklha, decided it would be safer for the Dalai Lama to skip the festival and remain inside the Jokhang Temple during his exams. So he announced that the Precious Protector was feeling unwell and wouldn't appear in public. At the same time, the Chinese government sent the Dalai Lama an invitation to attend a dance troupe performance at their headquarters after his exams. These two incidents sparked rumors and fears among Tibetans that the Dalai Lama's life was in danger.

The Monlam festival ended on March 4, and it was time for the Dalai Lama to return home to the Norbulingka Palace in the usual splendid procession. Seeing him parading through the streets settled the crowd for a time, though that wouldn't last for very long.

MARCH 5, 1959

TO YOUR HEALTH!

PRECIOUS PROTECTOR! PRECIOUS PROTECTOR!

HOW BLESSED WE ARE TO SEE YOU.

*Large, colorful butter sculptures created as offerings to the Buddha for the festival

I WISH I COULD HAVE WALKED AROUND THE FESTIVAL TO LOOK AT THE TORMA* AND PUPPET SHOWS.

PHUNTSOG TASHI TAKLHA DIDN'T THINK IT WOULD BE SAFE.

I UNDERSTAND. I'M GLAD TO BE FINISHED WITH MY EXAMS AND BACK HOME, ANYWAY. THE ROOMS IN THE JOKHANG ARE SO OLD AND DUSTY.

BEG PARDON, PRECIOUS PROTECTOR. THERE ARE CHINESE OFFICIALS HERE TO SEE YOU.

≡SIGH≡

SEND THEM TO THE THRONE ROOM, PLEASE.

LORD CHAMBERLAIN,* WAIT, WAIT!

*Also known as Phala Thupten Woden, one of the Dalai Lama's most trusted advisors

GOOD MORNING, KUSUNG DEPON. YOU'RE ALL OUT OF BREATH. WHAT'S THE MATTER?

I WAS JUST HAULED OFF TO BRIGADIER FU'S OFFICE TO TALK ABOUT THE PRECIOUS PROTECTOR'S ATTENDANCE AT THE DANCE RECITAL.

WHO IS BRIGADIER FU?

FU IS IN CHARGE OF THE PLA TROOPS IN LHASA. HE SAID THAT SINCE THE VENUE WAS INSIDE PLA HEADQUARTERS, THERE WOULD BE NO NEED FOR THE PRECIOUS PROTECTOR TO BE ACCOMPANIED BY HIS BODYGUARDS.

IF WE INSIST THAT HE MUST BE ACCOMPANIED, WE CAN ONLY SEND TWO TO THREE UNARMED PERSONNEL.

THAT IS PREPOSTEROUS.

NOT ONLY THAT, BUT HE CAN ONLY TRAVEL THERE BY A CAR THAT THE PLA SUPPLIES, ON A ROUTE GUARDED BY THE PLA. IF THE PRECIOUS PROTECTOR WANTS TO USE HIS OWN VEHICLE, HE COULD ONLY GO AS FAR AS THE KYICHU RIVER.

NONE OF IT IS ACCEPTABLE! WE NEED TO INFORM THE PRECIOUS PROTECTOR. NOW.

LATER IN THE DAY

...AND THOSE ARE THEIR TERMS.

HMMM.

WELL, YOUR HOLINESS?

MAYBE THIS ISN'T AS SERIOUS AS IT SOUNDS.

BUT—

EVERYTHING IS SET FOR TOMORROW, AND IT SEEMS LIKE A BAD IDEA, AND BAD MANNERS, TO CANCEL. WE'LL AGREE TO THEIR TERMS.

AS YOU WISH.

Tibetan Oracles

Many different cultures and religions have the concept of oracles. Usually an appointed person, such as a priest or priestess, acts as a medium that a god or goddess speaks through. People who want advice or wisdom from a divine source will consult the associated oracle. The person acting as the oracle usually goes into a mystical trance and channels the particular god who is being asked for advice.

In Tibet, the most important one is the Nechung Oracle, which has been around for hundreds of years. This oracle embodies Dorje Drakden, the protector god of Tibet and, therefore, it's the one that the Tibetan government mainly uses.

Besides the Nechung Oracle, the Dalai Lama also looks to the Gadong, Tenma, and Shugden oracles for guidance.

14

The Seventeen-Point Agreement

The "Seventeen-Point Agreement" (also known as the "Agreement of the Central People's Government and the Local Government of Tibet on Measures for the Peaceful Liberation of Tibet") was signed on May 23, 1951, by Chairman Mao Zedong. Mao believed that Tibet had been a part of China before and should be returned to its rightful owner once again. The agreement not only allowed the Chinese government to rule over Tibet, but also wanted Tibetan officials to actively assist in giving their national defense forces to the People's Liberation Army.

Tibetans have never recognized the agreement to be legitimate because, to them, Tibet had never been a part of China, and therefore could not be reabsorbed. Even though Tibetan officials were forced to sign it on May 23, 1951, Tibetans also never considered the document to be legal because the officials never brought their government seals (name stamps) with them. The seals used to stamp the document were copies made by the Chinese.

The agreement lasted until March 1959 when tens of thousands of Tibetans fought against the Chinese government. Cooperation between the two countries concluded with the Dalai Lama's escape to exile in India.

TWO DAYS LATER

I BEG YOUR PARDON FOR INTERRUPTING YOUR MEETING WITH THE KASHAG,* PRECIOUS PROTECTOR, BUT I HAVE A LETTER FROM THE PLA HEADQUARTERS.

IT'S FROM GENERAL TAN. HE WRITES, "IF YOU THINK IT NECESSARY AND POSSIBLE TO EXTRACT YOURSELF FROM YOUR PRESENT DANGEROUS SITUATION OF BEING HELD BY TRAITORS, WE CORDIALLY WELCOME YOU AND YOUR ENTOURAGE TO COME AND STAY FOR A SHORT TIME IN THE MILITARY AREA COMMAND."

STAY AT THE CHINESE GARRISON? UNDER THE SAME ROOF AS THE ENEMY?

WE MUST NOT THINK OF THEM AS THE ENEMY. OUR PEOPLE ARE AGITATED. GENERAL TAN IS UNDERSTANDABLY CONCERNED.

*The four-member council of ministers serving the Dalai Lama

PLEASE TELL THE LORD CHAMBERLAIN TO WRITE A REPLY TO GENERAL TAN FOR ME, TELLING HIM I FIND HIS SUGGESTION AGREEABLE.

YOU'RE SERIOUSLY CONSIDERING HIS REQUEST?

TO BE HONEST, I'VE NOT YET MADE UP MY MIND, BUT THERE IS NO HARM IN REASSURING GENERAL TAN THAT I APPRECIATE HIS CONCERN.

BRING THE LORD CHAMBERLAIN AND MY CHIEF OF MONASTIC STAFF TO ME IN THE THRONE ROOM.

LORD CHAMBERLAIN AND CHIKYAB KENPO, THE TIME FOR NEGOTIATING WITH THE CHINESE IS OVER. THE NECHUNG ORACLE INSISTS I'M TO FLEE TIBET FOR MY SAFETY AND THE SAFETY OF MY PEOPLE.

WHEN WILL YOU GO?

TONIGHT.

LORD CHAMBERLAIN, YOU WILL BE IN CHARGE OF GATHERING AND NOTIFYING EVERYONE WHO'LL BE IN THE ESCAPE PARTY.

YOUR FAMILY, OF COURSE, YOUR TUTORS, AND SOME MEMBERS OF THE COUNCIL...

CHIKYAB KENPO, YOU WILL MAKE PREPARATIONS—SECURING TRANSPORTATION, MONEY, SUPPLIES, AND SO ON.

PLEASE DON'T BREATHE A WORD OF THE PLAN TO ANYONE OUTSIDE OUR CLOSEST CIRCLE OF PEOPLE.

...YES, I KNOW THE SUN HAS YET TO RISE. BUT THERE ARE IMPORTANT TASKS TO DO.

YOU THREE ARE RESPONSIBLE FOR BRINGING OUR HORSES, MULES, AND DZOMOS* TO THE OTHER SIDE OF THE KYICHU RIVER WHERE YOU WILL TIE THEM UP TO GRAZE AND WATCH OVER THEM.

THEN YOU AND YOU...

*Also known as dzos; either a yak or a cross between a yak and a cow

...SEE TO IT THAT THE COOKS PREPARE AND PACKAGE A NUMBER OF FOODS THAT WILL KEEP FOR ABOUT TWO WEEKS OF TRAVEL...

...NEXT, THE TWO OF YOU ARE TO ALERT THE RESISTANCE FIGHTERS. HELP THEM COLLECT WEAPONS AND AMMUNITION AND TELL THEM TO WAIT WITH THE HORSES AND PACK ANIMALS ON THE OTHER SIDE OF THE KYICHU...

...AND I WILL WITHDRAW FUNDS— A VARIETY OF GOLD AND MONIES—FROM THE TREASURY.

28

Lord Chamberlain

Even though the Dalai Lama is known as "Precious Protector," Tibetans also try to keep *him* under protection. Not only do they want to shield him from any physical danger, because they also consider him the living embodiment of Buddha, and therefore a god, they also want to spare him the daily grind and toil that ordinary humans endure.

To do that, Tibetans created a court of personal attendants consisting of upper status monks. And the head of this court, in the highest-ranking position below the Dalai Lama, is the Lord Chamberlain (otherwise known as Phala). Three clerical aides (the Kenpos) help the Lord Chamberlain supervise the personal attendants in ensuring that the Dalai Lama's needs with respect to food, daily living, and religious ceremony are met.

Phala Thupten Woden served as the 14th Dalai Lama's Lord Chamberlain during the period covered in this book. Having accompanied the Precious Protector on his escape from Lhasa, Lord Chamberlain never got to see his homeland again. He died in 1985.

ARE THE LEADERS OF THE REBEL CROWDS STILL MILLING AROUND OUTSIDE THE PALACE GATES?

THE POPULAR LEADERS, YOUR HOLINESS? YES, THEY ARE.

PLEASE GATHER THEM AND BRING THEM TO MY THRONE ROOM. I WOULD LIKE TO HAVE A WORD WITH THEM.

THANK YOU FOR MEETING WITH ME. I WOULD LIKE TO ASK A FAVOR OF YOU.

OF COURSE, PRECIOUS PROTECTOR. YOU KNOW WE WOULD DO ANYTHING FOR YOU!

THEN I WILL SWEAR YOU TO ABSOLUTE SECRECY. PROMISE YOU WON'T BREATHE A WORD OF WHAT I'M ABOUT TO TELL YOU TO ANYONE.

ON THE ADVICE OF THE ORACLE, I WILL LEAVE TONIGHT AND SEEK SANCTUARY IN INDIA.

TONIGHT?!

IT'S ONLY A TEMPORARY MEASURE. I INTEND TO BE BACK AS SOON AS IT'S SAFE TO DO SO. I WANT YOU TO BEG THE CROWD TO NOT PROVOKE THE PLA, FOR THEIR OWN SAFETY. UNDERSTOOD?

WE... UNDERSTAND.

GOOD. THANK YOU, AND GO IN PEACE.

31

YES, THAT'S IT... TAKE IT SLOWLY AND STEADILY, PRECIOUS PROTECTOR.

WHOOOAAA.

EASY. EEEEASY.

GLAD THAT'S DONE. WHERE TO NEXT?

Tibet བོད།
The Land of the Snow Lion

Located at the center of East, South, and Inner Asia, Tibet has the greatest elevation of any country on earth, with Mount Everest being its (and the world's) highest peak. While people have lived in the Tibetan Plateau since at least twenty-one thousand years ago, Tibet as an empire, or country, didn't form until the seventh century. Since then, it's been the ancestral homeland to the Tibetan people along with other ethnic groups such as the Monpa, Tamang, Qiang, Sherpa, and Lhoba.

Many people of Tibet are subsistence farmers and herders, meaning they grow food to feed only their own families, and not to sell or export. Tibetans have also adopted the majestic, mythical Snow Lion as their emblem. This creature not only represents the snowy mountain peaks surrounding the country, but also symbolizes strength, power, fearlessness, and joy.

Throughout the centuries, Tibet and China have gone through many diplomatic eras, some friendly and some warring. Unfortunately for the 14th Dalai Lama, it is during the troubled, warring times that he has had to rule.

43

WHAT IS IT? IS EVERYTHING ALL RIGHT?

I'M AFRAID WE BEAR BAD NEWS.

THE PLA HAS ATTACKED LHASA. OFFICIALS AND OTHERS WHO ARE ACCUSED OF BEING ANTI-CHINESE HAVE BEEN ARRESTED AND ARE BEING PUBLICLY HUMILIATED.

THEY'VE ALSO FIRED COUNTLESS GUNS AND CANNONS AT THE NORBULINGKA AND MANY OTHER BUILDINGS IN LHASA.

I WAS A FOOL TO THINK IT WAS POSSIBLE TO NEGOTIATE AND LIVE PEACEABLY WITH MAO AND THE PLA. WE *MUST* OFFICIALLY SEVER ALL TIES WITH THEM. AS SOON AS WE REACH THE LHUNTSÉ DZONG, I WILL MAKE THE DECLARATION.

45

47

THE NEXT MORNING...

I...I DON'T FEEL WELL.

I'LL FETCH LORD CHAMBERLAIN.

GOOD MORNING, PRECIOUS PROTECTOR. WE'RE PREPARING TO PACK UP CAMP.

I AM AFRAID YOUR FEVER HAS SPIKED, AND IT LOOKS LIKE YOU MIGHT HAVE DYSENTERY. WE MUST STAY PUT UNTIL YOU ARE BETTER.

BUT WE CAN'T DELAY. WE'RE SO CLOSE.

YOU'RE IN NO SHAPE TO TRAVEL. WE WILL STAY ONE MORE NIGHT. I'LL SEE IF I CAN FIND A LESS LEAKY PLACE FOR YOU TO REST IN.

YOU WILL HELP ME MOVE HIM TO A DRIER SPOT ONCE I FIND IT.

YES, LORD CHAMBERLAIN.

...ONE OF OUR SOURCES TELLS US THAT THE DALAI LAMA HAS FOOLISHLY FALLEN OFF HIS HORSE, SERIOUSLY INJURING HIMSELF!
HA HA HA!
WHAT'S WRONG, YOUR HOLINESS?
I DIDN'T MEAN TO SCARE YOU. THERE ARE VERY SILLY RUMORS ABOUT ME ON THE RADIO CONCERNING MY DISAPPEARANCE.
ALL RIGHT, THEN...
LAUGHING MAKES ME FEEL BETTER. THANK YOU FOR YOUR CLEVER IDEA TO BRING ME THE RADIO.

54

57

58

Conclusion

The people of India welcomed the Dalai Lama as an honored guest and gave him a new home. He and his group settled first in Mussoorie, then permanently in Dharamsala, India, where tens of thousands more Tibetans joined them, fleeing from persecution back in their home country. Without the Dalai Lama in Tibet, life became very harsh for Tibetans who remained behind. They were, and still are, subjected to violence, starvation, and public humiliation by the Chinese government.

Dharamsala became the headquarters of the Dalai Lama's exiled government. He drafted a new constitution with laws appropriate to their adopted home and situation. His goal was to establish a democratically elected government for Tibetans, something that Tibet had never had before. The Dalai Lama realized the plan's success depended on educating his people, both to learn about the wider world and to remember their own culture. So, he founded a school which taught Tibetan language, dance, and music, along with regular subjects like math, social studies, and science.

During the 1970s, the Dalai Lama traveled to Europe, the United States, and Canada. Later, he would journey even farther. Not only did he want to experience the world firsthand, but he also wanted to spread word about the challenges Tibet faced under hostile foreign rule. Everywhere he went, he shared his Buddhist philosophy of nonviolent protest and kindness. This philosophy is embodied in one of his favorite prayers:

> *For as long as space endures,*
> *And for as long as living beings remain,*
> *Until then may I, too, abide*
> *To dispel the misery of the world.*

Because of his tireless efforts, the Dalai Lama and Tibet are now internationally known. In 1989, when he was fifty-four years old, he was awarded the Nobel Peace Prize for his work and his message of peace.

The fateful decision to escape in March 1959 made a world of difference—and a difference to the world.

Timeline of the 14th Dalai Lama's Life

1935 — The Dalai Lama is born on July 6 in the small village of Takster, Tibet, and named Lhamo Thondup

1939 — Arrives on October 8 in Lhasa with his family after being proclaimed the 14th Dalai Lama

1940 — Officially enthroned as the Dalai Lama on February 22

1950 — China's People's Liberation Army invades Tibet on October 7

1951 — The Seventeen-Point Agreement is signed on May 23

1959 — Protests erupt against China's People's Liberation Army, as the army begins to attack villages in Tibet

— The Dalai Lama flees the country

— Crosses into India on March 31

1960 — Settles in Dharamsala, India, on April 30, where he establishes a school and a new Tibetan government

1987 — Puts forth the Five-Point Peace Plan to the US Congress's Human Rights Caucus, on September 21, addressing how to establish protections for Tibet

1989 — Selected to receive the Nobel Peace Prize in October "for advocating peaceful solutions based upon tolerance and mutual respect in order to preserve the historical and cultural heritage of his people"

2011 — Steps down as the political leader of Tibet on March 19

Bibliography

*Books for young readers

Ginsburgs, George, and Michael Mathos. "Tibet's Administration in the Transition Period, 1951–1954." *Pacific Affairs*, vol. 32, no. 2 (1959): 162–177. https://doi.org/10.2307/2753562.v.

Gyatso, Tenzin. *Freedom in Exile: The Autobiography of the Dalai Lama*. New York: HarperCollins, 1990.

Norman, Alexander. *The Dalai Lama: An Extraordinary Life*. Boston: Houghton Mifflin Harcourt, 2020.

*Rau, Dana Meachen. *Who Is the Dalai Lama?* New York: Penguin Workshop, 2018.

Tethong, Tenzin Geyche, and Gautam Pemmaraju. *His Holiness the Fourteenth Dalai Lama: An Illustrated Biography*. Northampton, MA: Interlink Books, 2021.

Website

www.dalailama.com

Teresa Robeson is the APALA Award-winning author of *Queen of Physics: How Wu Chien Shiung Helped Unlock the Secrets of the Atom* (also ILA Nonfiction Picture Book Honor and NCTE Orbis Pictus Nonfiction Recommended Book). Other publications include *Two Bicycles in Beijing* and an essay in *Nonfiction Writers Dig Deep*, edited by Melissa Stewart. Teresa lives with her scientist-professor husband, younger son, and a motley crew of chickens on their twenty-seven-acre mini homestead. Learn more about her work at teresarobeson.com.

Angela Poon is a freelance illustrator and comic artist living in Mississauga, Ontario. She is a graduate of Sheridan College's Bachelor of Illustration program, and is the illustrator of Deborah Kerbel's graphic novel *Fred & Marjorie: A Doctor, a Dog, and the Discovery of Insulin*. Angela enjoys capturing warmth and little moments of everyday life in her illustrations. Find more of her work at angela-poon.com.